JUMP SCARE

JUMP SCARE

POEMS

DANIEL ZOMPARELLI

TALONBOOKS

Talonbooks
9259 Shaughnessy Street, Vancouver, British Columbia, Canada V6P 6R4
talonbooks.com

Talonbooks is located on xʷməθkʷəy̓əm, Sḵwx̱wú7mesh, and səlilwətał Lands.

First printing: 2024

Typeset in Arno
Printed and bound in Canada on 100% post-consumer recycled paper

Talonbooks acknowledges the financial support of the Canada Council for the Arts, the Government of Canada through the Canada Book Fund, and the Province of British Columbia through the British Columbia Arts Council and the Book Publishing Tax Credit.

Canadä Canada Council Conseil des arts BRITISH BRITISH COLUMBIA
for the Arts du Canada COLUMBIA ARTS COUNCIL
An agency of the Province of British Columbia

Library and Archives Canada Cataloguing in Publication

Title: Jump scare : poems / Daniel Zomparelli.
Names: Zomparelli, Daniel, 1985– author.
Identifiers: Canadiana 2023049823X | ISBN 9781772016109 (softcover)
Classification: LCC PS8649.O66 J86 2024 | DDC C811/.6—dc23

FOR SOMEONE,

I HOPE

EXISTENCE IS HONESTLY SO EMBARRASSING

NOBODY!

for Emily Dickinson

we can be nobody here
we can disappear, it's so very easy
drink champagne

we can sit in the corner
and no one asks us to be anything
here it is all very easy!

Emily, I have been to Disneyland
a desert city turned make-believe
what a mirage I can see

in Hollywood you can
drink champagne and easily
forget a name

Emily, did you know (of course you know, you told me)
that it is so easy to disappear
David Blaine my ass into thin air!

I drink champagne
and Emily, I know I should be talking to Frank
I should be talking to him I know

but I want to be nobody
to forget my own name
like a Hollywood exec

when I order a martini at Little Dom's
I ask, "do you know who I am?"
they reply "no," and I yell, "exactly!"

to be somebody
to be known
what a fucking sight

I'd much rather be the ghost
who haunts Griffith Park
in the dead of night

ALGORITHM IS GONNA GET YOU

HOW TO GET WASHBOARD ABS – FAST!

you keep saying / you're from the future but your bmw is a '95 and I
can't even fucking let go of the past.

the guy who designed crop tops
has all of our money, let's get him. //

the economy will be saved with same-sex
themed wedding cakes. // don't ask / don't tell / don't miss out on
this offer / and for the next three minutes
we'll throw in a second slap chop for free. //

wait, wait, wait, are you a jack gay or a will gay? // wait, wait, on the
old one or the reboot? // meet me at the corner of commerce and gay
culture, you get the best g there. // have you planned your gaycation
yet?

dildos can't hug you at night, but they fill the void. // innovation is
the reproduction of a butthole in the shape of a flashlight. I would
shine a light out for you. / can you great gatsby the light and flesh it
over here.

73 percent of american homes have been designed by two gay men on reality shows that were cancelled years ago. // I no longer have to look for gay subtext because it's easy to digest now. / I can't sell myself out anymore because I no longer fill
a diversity quotient. we don't talk about *glee* anymore. // I bought the barcelona chair. ate beef wellington
and cried bear tears at pottery barn.

american apparel supports gay marriage [1] and all I got was this lousy shirt. // bears and boners
over bedding. // don't quit your gay job, you will need that when the gay depression hits and you are left
without a gay penny to your gay name.

you might be a sad / middle-aged wife / who gets no respect / has lost all confidence / can't get a job, lost / a son, and can't afford / clothes, but rupaul / will help you
at 8 p.m. / pacific standard time. [2]

Jockstrapped to my work. // we tried to use ky his and hers, [3]
but we didn't know who should use what.

I bought this because I wanted to have washboard abs
and the guy in the magazine
has washboard abs. // I think he's hot because he looks like
he would beat me up, and I'm really
into guys who look like they'll beat me up. // what about
the gay's gaze? // rock hudson /
and a pack of smokes. // gun-oil lube spilled all over my ex's floor
and they're both still slippery
after all these years!

I calvin kleined my way to the top.

---

1   Gay Marriage is just marriage now, but expensive.
2   Cancelled.
3   Formerly "KY Him and Her" and now "KY Yours and Mine."

ctrl+alt+delete // me // drag and drop it into the folder. // undo drag
// I've been using the crystal method.
// unfrienemy // don't worry, I'll just retweet it.
// you put the homo in homeowner. // poke.[1] / do you think he's
sexier than me? // cheat day!

tenderqueers brought beanie babies back and for that I cannot
forgive them.

what happens when several men who work out all the time move onto
a magical island where there is a shortage of t-shirts?
find out next week on outtv. // viewer discretion is advised as
this show will be cancelled after one season. // a gay vampire show is
a little too offensive for me
but I'll bite. // the british lady is reaming out the token gay guy about
the token black girl
on *housewives of d.c.*[2]

the greatest gay love story was on a series about prisoners.[3] // he
looks sleepy, does he bump?

I have a blog. I have a gay blog. I have an activist-oriented gay blog. I
have a porn-activist-orientated gay art blog.
I have a tumblr[4] account. butt: unplugged.

god hates a lot of things.

---

1 No one pokes anymore.
2 Cancelled.
3 *The Last of Us* has since made the greatest gay love story.
4 No one uses Tumblr anymore (actually it's making a comeback).

I never want to go to a grocery store and figure out which coffee bean is the most ethical to buy. why does possibility feel like a trap?

gay guys don't use edible chocolate oil for romantic massages. // I was never very fierce. // no one is ever gay in a disney film except maybe the fussy clock in *beauty and the beast* and now I guess that guy in *beauty and the beast* live action who just winks and nods at a man. //

big gay al / cam and mitchell / chandler's dad / holt / but not lenny and carl /zaaappp. // we've reached that point of progress where they can have evil white gays on every tv show now!

the twinkie defence. twitter said twink death and I said r.i.p. to my bodyodyody! /// perpetually jaded, I hate being from the future. / fuck you society, said the tattoo that I ordered off amazon. / if you're looking for me, I'll be under the rainbow-balloon arch during the pride parade in the speedos and airbrushed toyota logo. / mazda miata my medulla oblongata / he overdosed / on liberation.

his-and-his stemware collection, charge it! / guncle Disney collection, charge it! gays for guns t-shirts for sale on etsy dot com, charge it! okrrrrr // did i buy the right thing to get me out of my depression?

stanley tucci and colin firth have had more gay sex than me. I want to
repackage queer trauma.
queer trauma is straight now.

love, simon, have you heard of her? *call me by your name?* actually, I
can't call anyone / my iphone broke.

I'm goop'ed and gagged and bound by the terms of this agreement.

I wonder how much queer trauma you can cash in on / because I'm
still in queer debt. I process my trauma
through the peloton community. push push those pedals to pedestals.
you're looking fit / you're looking fun / your credit card has expired!

do you like flipping the pages of this book so quickly?

are you worried it's capitalism destroying your attention span?

every one of my insta ads is for designer anxiety meds. panic / but
make it fashion / at the disco. monetize that! // please help, my tweet
has gone viral.

if you see aaron schock's cock at a peter thiel party are you complicit?
// the new fracking challenge on *rupaul's drag race* is sending me / I
literally love the way the earth crumbles under my feet.

I'm too ugly for an onlyfans but not smart enough to be a twitter
influencer so I just started writing poems no one wants. I unfollowed
every hot person on insta as a political act / they didn't notice.

straight people call everything porn / straight people are grooming
you for consumption / straight people love groom culture / groom
this / groom that / but never two grooms.

I bought his cosmetics because I didn't think he's a white supremacist. white supremacists rebranded themselves by shopping at the business casual side of the gap. Did you fall into the gap? // I WAS IN THE AMAZON PRIME OF MY LIFE

an algorithm shaped my personality and I bought everything it said to and here I am, a nightmare on west elm street. // I spent most of my life savings on sexy underwear and I still have no self-esteem.
I tried to get the self-esteem but the lineup was so long and it cut into a supreme shop.

my algorithm is still trying to figure out my gender / bitch / catch me if you can.

honestly, my body dysmorphia is fucking glowing. / if god hates fags so much then why did he give us all of the good drugs and snappy comebacks? thanos snap me out of existence please. bend and snap / this anxiety attack.

the economy has collapsed! oh please, the economy, we love you, get up!

for a couple of years white gay guys were getting nazi haircuts and I want to unpack that / we bought von dutch hats until the guys who beat us up bought von dutch hats / we bought republic jeans until the guys who beat us up bought republic jeans / we bought fred perry polo shirts until the guys who beat us up bought fred perry polo shirts. Is this outfit gonna beat me up in two years? What's the return policy here?

I used to believe I would be the rebellious queer who would go down swinging, but lately I am just scrolling / liking your posts.

macklemored from the perspective of intent. Intent is.

we keep tweeting about different things. I'm sharing the video of a hot cop dancing at pride to show that there is peace in the world / cops show their love by spraying pepper in your eyes awwwww. your prison industrial complex is showing!!

western capitalism eats everything, it's all "nom nom nom, haha / anyway buy my nom nom shirt, link in bio."

freedom is the choice of not drinking the brand of vodka that pulled its ad from the pride parade. if there is no ethical consumption under capitalism, then I better chick-fil-a / but not on a sunday. I want to make a joke about masks and mascs but if I did I would literally cause a pandemic. boycott with the boys. girlcott with the girlies.

used to fuck in bathroom stalls and now you do / it in your six-hundred-square foot condo / before 9 p.m. because / the strata has been concerned about / noise levels. I hetero-organized this event. wait, are you at the cis-het quarters? // the token gay guy on *big brother* never wins. [1] // I'm sorry, ma'am, your husband has been / queer / eyed. as you can see here, he's got the french tuck // in the reboot, the *queer eye* crew is here to neoliberalize your home!!!! // weird how I never saw you at the club before / dumbledore.

I went on *queer eye* and all I got was a recipe for guacamole and a one-on-one with my abuser.

you keep saying you're from the future but I am still here in the past / doomscrolling twitter / where the future no longer exists / linking to a soundcloud song called yassss queen she works to death. if only this death drop could save me from extermination.

at a certain point, someone will ask you if you are on antidepressants and you won't know the answer / but you will know the brand henny.

---

1   A gay guy has since won *Big Brother.*

I LITERALLY FEEL BAD ALL OF THE TIME LOL

Do you like the sound of fireworks or do they create a sense of urgency in your gut? Do you like this party that consumes you? You haven't spoken to anyone, would you like to ghost? Did you ask anyone else a question? Did you compliment the host? Did the lights make you dizzy again? Are you embarrassed? Are you still on your phone? Did you notice that crack in the bathroom mirror? Did you wonder where it came from? Did you visualize your head hitting against it to make that same crack deepen? Did you shake off that negative thought? Did you eat anything? Did you drink too much? Did you laugh at the wrong thing? Are you having fun yet? Do you need me to call you a cab? Does your body feel like stone? Can you work in the morning?

It's been one week in your bed
told everyone you were sick, lie

about the way your body turns
to wood, skin varnished.

You can't explain that doors are portals
to another dimension, cars like whales

slop you up, easier to say "I feel sick"
the way your dad calls it "sick."

Your dad claims the family got this
from a curse brought back from Italy

malocchio, now you feel safer inside like
a poem that claims "you" instead of "I."

All you can do is watch YouTube
find out how everything is made.

Your insides are moving pieces
small cogs, clicking. At least Pinocchio was a real boy.

Leaving is a never-ending process
you have to leave your home

you have to come back to leave again
make sure to actually walk out the door.

You wonder if you die on the way home
who will clean out the lint in your dryer.

Think about how your nose got so
big telling everyone you're fine.

You watched *Maleficent* and thought about how
angry you look when you're quiet.

He asked you what book you were reading, and it
was a poetry book by someone who ended up being an alleged abuser.

You ordered a dessert to linger around him, ate dense
chocolate while the man behind talked about

his colonoscopy. Colonoscopies are the quickest way
to a man's heart, so everyone falls in love with doctors.

He laughed. You became nervous, gave a thumbs up
to everything he asked, even questions you should have

answered. You left without saying goodbye, fading back into
the dark forest you came from, Diablo on your shoulder.

You want to do something fun but it's raining
and you forget what fun is.

Put all of your memories in Mason jars
every one of them, label them.

In a jar, put the time you said depression wasn't funny
to a group of strangers at a party.

In another jar, put the time you squealed so loud everyone
in the school assembly heard.

"Do you struggle to maintain
friendships?" Text your friends

but don't make plans with them
just see what they are doing.

Stop the fucking wind chimes
outside from clanging.

Think of death to feel better because it feels
like a break from feeling bad.

> *click-clack zzzzz flash zzzz*
> *muscle tendon blur you're*
>
> *a demon, cut slice crunch*
> *jaw cut cement floor crack*

Find out if McDonald's doesn't mould after being left
on your counter for several weeks. It doesn't!

Cut out all of the letter *i*'s from the book you're reading
for an art project you'll never finish.

Sweep all your hair into a corner.
Silence the wind chimes.

Disorder the things in your life from greatest to weakest

including all of your personality traits.

Stubborn. Attentive to detail. Problem solver. Focused. Kind of funny.
Easily confused. Repetitive. Emotionally cold. Distant. Downer.
Killjoy. Critical. Repetitive. Easily confused.

"Is your memory
like steel?"

Fester on a memory too long
move all of your furniture.

Laugh
at a dog taking a shit.

> *eeeeeh flicker a light out*
> *make a tooth split burn*
>
> *an image dewdrops on grass*
> *fizzle out find a forest*

"Do people call you a
robot?"

Meditate. Let the gentle sounds of cars honking outside
rush over your slowly decaying body.

Medicate. Let a pill
take you away.

"Do you prefer a quiet place
alone?"

Call all of the ghosts to the front
of the living room. Request them

to recite their lives backwards starting
with you.

Duct tape the neighbour's wind chimes

to your favourite tree.

nobody can see you if you are
nobody at all

make yourself as small as possible
until you are barely there

The coyote comes again
to ensure another sleepless night

their face lit by the automatic light
you stare up at them in your underwear

and wonder if they are staring at you
questioning those tiny briefs

the light flickers in the backyard
and the coyote stands still, you tell them

this is my house, please stop taking
my dog's toys and ripping them apart

but maybe the coyote is thinking
this is my home you are on

and thank you for the toys, they
rip so nicely in my mouth.

You think about the woman who wore too many beads
she smiled brightly in a detox centre.

She said she loved collecting beads
the way they rattled when she moved, she floated

when she spoke, did the beads weigh her down or
did she use them to anchor her to the floor?

You put rocks on your father-in-law's gravestone
each to say hello. Your husband put stones

in the garden beds in hopes a spell
could make them grow.

Would a bead help anchor to the floor
not this drink, not this cigarette?

Your father claims none of this is real, he's always floating
well beyond reach, reality is a burden to some.

You wish that you could carry all these beads
so that you don't worry, you too will fly away.

Now dreams are more vivid
you dreamed your mouth

was full of pebbles that rattled
around instead of teeth. If you are real

please blink twice, place a pebble on your lips
to feel better about tomorrow.

Place a bead or a small rock on the earth
put a spell on time to slow it down.

Are you still awake?

Your husband buzzes your hair in the bathtub again
and all memories are present, including the time one of the stars

from *Dead Like Me* called you a loser for dumping
your ex, who then punched a wall that night, fracturing

bones, much like the memory itself. Break
down because you clipped your dog's nail too close

to the quick, and it bled out all over the rug
bleed out nightmares every night like Gwyneth Paltrow

ruining Christmas at your dead mother's house
or him falling back into heroin, or

Lena Denham ruining the last wedge of parmigiana.
Worry about your mental health because sometimes

the brain is static and buzz and crackles and noise like
flick flick, a lighter, flick, memory, crack skull bone blur.

But the blood spurted out
from your dog's nail and you apologized

over and over again as if to say, "I'm sorry. I promise I will try not to
fall into a mental breakdown that leaves you burdened to

take care of me, and I love you which means I now have another
thing to be anxious about, and

sorry about the voices I hear and call them ghosts, or that I let
Lena Dunham take charge of the kitchen"

you've said this before to him
fearful of becoming the Mad Hatter, terrorizing
with large hats and teacups from too many mixed sets

he says, "I don't worry about that
there isn't a version of you I can't imagine not loving," as he sweeps
our hair in the tub, balling it into a tumbleweed.

How come everyone is a real estate agent? You sold a home
to the woods, the woods sold the home back, the woods said
it's a pretty great deal bro congrats, prices skyrocket
so you join an MLM and sell creams made out of your
body. Creams that cake instead of absorb, this poem
is an MLM do you want a sample?
Spend the rest of your evenings
watching *Guy's Diners, Drive-Ins and Dives* because it's the only
thing that calms the brain. If you think these things don't
relate, then well, you could be right. The psychologist writes another note
while you describe another episode. She also writes a note
when you say popcorn is bad, and that you tend to make
connections to unrelated things like a constellation. You think about what
Guy Fieri worries about at night, what keeps him from slumber.
Guy Fieri doesn't like to eat eggs, is it the texture or taste?
You can't eat eggs cooked certain ways because of the texture.
Guy flips the egg aside from the burger or chilaquiles
it flops over onto the counter. Is it flip or flop?
"Flip or Flop" is your go-to username
because *Flip or Flop* was on TV once
while you were signing up for a game on your phone
but it's no longer available, try again.
You wish ghosts would be more vocal or less shy.
You wish you could fall asleep.
You wish you could text every person you met to ask if they are
OK, if they have seen this episode too, even if they died
ask them how's the afterlife, are there smash burgers there, let them know
you are OK too, you guess. You would tell them how
the psychologist diagnosed you with autism and brought up
your obsession with Triple D, you'd say you're not great
but not bad, like a restaurant Guy Fieri would go to
and say it was taking him to flavour town.
On this episode Guy is going to his hometown, a place
you stayed in one night at a haunted hotel. You were up
all night hoping to see a ghost, but instead
stared into the one-street downtown, lights blaring all night.

poems are not supposed to stare at you
directly in the eyes

they are more quiet than that, they can't
socialize the way others do

poems are more about full bear hugs
and pressing your body against earth

to see what shape you make in the dirt
or how the grass bends under your weight

poems can be as direct as you need
instructive, focused, maybe too focused

poems are there for you
but sometimes they're not

this poem is a stimming tool
when chaos brain returns

keep this poem in case of sensory overload
keep this poem for when the world

feels like a pulsing vein
take a breath, you're OK.

                                        Did you lock the front door?

your husband comes home with an olive tree
and plants it in a pot near the front window
it has a stake to hold it up
too weak to stand on its own

                                        Did you have your coffee yet?

he tends to it as you tend to
memories, the whir in your brain
burnout keeps you firmly
planted in bed

                                   Did you find a way to let that memory go?

your husband takes the dog for a walk
and comes back with flyers
from white supremacists, they papered
our neighbourhood with antisemitic propaganda

                              Did you become something you never expected?

they used zip-lock bags
with tiny pebbles to throw them onto
each lawn, how many rocks to weigh
down hate

                                        Did you respond to that text?

your husband asks if it's too soon
to take the stake out from the olive tree
you say maybe tomorrow
it will hold itself on its own

è tutto a posto?

he bought an olive tree
to ground your new home
one day maybe the roots will
break through the pot, the floor

Did you remember to lock the front door?

the infrastructure, grow large enough
to live in, a house on a tree
blooming from the dirt
with pebbles at the door.

Your mother made you by the shore
of the ocean, out of rocks, sand, litter
a heart made of pogs
lungs of cigarette butts
skin of plastic and condoms
heart with a broken watch, tick
tick, tick, ticking every moment.

You made your way from
the ocean, learned to walk
and run and speak as well
but never how to swim.

You told everyone you were real
but they could hear your heart tick
tick, ticking in a way
impossible to disguise.

You did everything to hide the tick
eventually discarding the watch
into the ocean.

One day it was
swallowed up by a whale
when you weren't keeping
watch.

You did your best to not be slopped
up, but the ocean is rising and the tick
tick, tick, it calls for you.

The whale beckons, says
only you can get it
out.

                                        voui entrare?

si, apri la bocca

HOLD ON TO THE GRIEF, IT'S ALL THAT'S LEFT

HE DRAGS HER BODY, OR WORKING BACKWARDS

In memory of Tina Zomparelli and Simira Zomparelli

"She's gone."

When I walk out into the cold, I pretend that you call to tell me to bundle up and watch out for the icy streets.

///

How do you name the file of the obituary, type blah because blah is blah, we enter the static. My tenses are wrong. When we / my tenses are wrong / when we / it's not like I told you / enter the static. / She's. / When we full circle / sleep / slip / press / chemo / press / in lieu. / Keep calm. / Would you like to see her one last time before we take her away? / Just like you. / You will feel / blank / blank / blank / blank. Smouldering / blood cell / this is not what she looked like. She's   was. / There are no words, I'm sure you are hearing this a lot, but there are no words, words words words words words I'm sorry words words words words words.

It was all of the pills pills pills pills pills pills pills
                        mon tues wed thurs fri sat sun / IV drip drip drip
        dream dream dream you can't be here / at an eighty-foot dinner table,
            this dinner is for you, your last supper, in here, there's three of you,
        each wearing your favourite outfit, smiling and telling me everything
            is going to be fine, and here, breathe, you fix dinner, breathe, and
        here the IV drip drip, breathe, and here you appear and appear and
        appear and appear until I ask you to stop. Until I tell you it makes the
        morning too unbearable. / Blink, fester, await the sun. / Rip red gems
        from a pomegranate, you need to eat something, you're wasting away.
                                        / When we blister.

        Dear Mother, the nightmares won't stop. / Sleep, rest, await the sun.

\\\

        You came back and everything was fine. Your heart was better and
        we lived in your mother's house now. When you walked out of the
            kitchen, I remembered that you are dead and I plastic myself.

///

Warfarin coumadin discharge displace allergy decussate cap glycerine sup chemo sennosides tab allopurinol bone marrow bortezomib

blood test drink liquids sterility blood transfusion smouldering
myeloma modicum loperamide acetaminophen tylenol white blood
cells platelets cut burn asa for your heart advil bone swell sweat no
more sweets Mom taste alteration transplant to do numbness hair
loss fluid bleed dexamethasone mimics lanolin induced coumadin
dilantin store do not density decadrone dexasone hexadrol cyborg
cyclophosphamide vomit bladder lanolin cycle cytoxan colchicine
sorry procytox someone else's heart.

\\\

    The monster, burned to black ash, was waiting for me inside his cage.
        I told you he would get out, but you were certain he was trapped.
                When you looked away, he escaped.

///

I buried all the monsters in the backyard
but your mom is dead the words
they are waiting, so I buried all
the monsters in the backyard
but the monsters they
rise your mom is dead, I buried
all the monsters in the yard and you
said making friends was easy. I
buried all the monsters in the backyard
but your mom is dead, the words.

///

Everything will be fine.
It's fine. .
I'm fine.
I'm doing fine.
It's going to be fine.
Fine.
I'm fine.
We're fine.
It's fine here.
It was fine.

Fine.
Everything will be fine.
Fine then.
You're fine.
No thanks, I'm fine.
I'm fine, I don't need anything.
I feel fine today.
I feel fine.
Fine.

///

Pills are for a polite nation, quiet yourself, with the yellow one. Come to think of it, you didn't know me very well. I was the one who lit the dark with flower petals, who soaked the pillows with tears and blamed it on the nightmares. Years later your name burned itself into my back in blood ink. Can't figure out how to scrub it off, so I lettered it through the alphabet. Language doesn't gift me anymore, it burrows under the eyelids, like the prayers Mother sent you. Did you get them? They're under the front-door mat, let yourself in.

///

Kiss pictures like saying hello to death.

\\\

There's an endless amount of rooms with endless amounts of doors, and in each room there is you, but you're different each time. Wearing white and smiling, wearing red and dancing, with an apron cooking pasta, and as many doors as I open, you're there, waiting. And I tell you to stop, to let me be, and yet each door I open, you are there. And you are there and you are there and I can't say goodbye and you are there. And the doors continue to open.

///

You asked me why I was tired, and it was too much to tell you that the one I loved more than anyone else had broken my heart, and you were sad because I couldn't smile. We sat quietly as our hearts pressed against our chests, yours skipping every second beat.

\\\

You told me to go upstairs to change. I found a small suitcase of my clothes. I had nothing to wear. I pulled the clothes out in a desperate fashion. I ripped them from the suitcase but there was nothing to wear. I couldn't breathe. Nothing would work. Nothing felt right. The clothes would never fit.

///

Telephone call
"She's gone."

///

Maybe you were wondering why I always smelled of tequila or beer.
I sat in the hospital chapel the night you told me about your first
boyfriend. I didn't know where else to go. It felt like everyone in the
city had left. All that was left was cement and glass.

///

"As kids mature into teens
they start to understand
that every human being
eventually dies, regardless
of grades, behaviour, wishes
or anything they try to do."

///

I can't get any more tattoos, I'm running out of body to talk about.

///

The failed pedagogics
of "I love you."

///

They said, "Rest in peace," but
I drag her body wherever I go.

\\\

We were shopping for groceries. You wanted to make sure my fridge
was full. I was happy to see you again. It's been so long. Death has
made you distant.

///

You ask if I'm mad at you
like I have been fuming

all night, but I am tired and death
is still stink upon our shirts
where you can't see the pain
of goodbye on my lips still
so you ask if I'm mad at you
like this has anything to do
with us, and wetness dabs below
your eyes, and I start to scream
and you ask why I'm mad, but I
can't put words together
like he can't reverse time or fix
a severed spine but you
will leave me, so we hold
tight to each other with one foot
out the door because it's the only
way we know how to love
as long as we don't use the word
or as long as we separate it from I and you
or this
is always about us

///

When your daughter passed away, the dark came. I inhaled cherry
blossoms. I would sneak into your bed and hide under the covers.
She can't protect me anymore, just as you can't now. The nightmares
returned, please wake me up.

///

Sometimes the world shifts and I change
small details. Apples taste like pears now
and my arms are much bigger than
they were, you say everything and I listen.

                    Sometimes the world shifts and the past changes
                        we made it to Christmas, I fried us zeppole,
                        I told you about my nightmares, and the one
                            about Gwyneth Paltrow made you laugh.

\\\

You said you were going to Mexico for a trip, and I waited for your
return.

///

Feel the thump of body
against weight
against metal
hoods
against glass
windshields
or feel sixty kilometres
per hour against flesh
against
bones
against
what you didn't say
see death
per hour.

///

I was trying to breathe
but I put words instead
of air so they blocked the throat.
Pull off the road
you can't see.
Like a fissure
necessary, like say
you're sorry like
why are you always alone?

///

She calls again, she is driving towards the Apocalypse. The world is
being consumed. She says she is sorry, she took the wrong turn and is
driving right into the destruction.

///

Pull over.
I said fucking pull over.

///

"Your father
used to scream
at me if I drove him past the funeral
like I was going to kill him
and leave him on the doorstep. But
we all have fantasies."

"She's gone."

"10. Simply experience your anxiety for forty-five minutes." –
There is this and that and this and that and this and that and this and
that and this and that and this and that and this and that and this and
that and this and that and this and that and this and that and this and
that and this and that and this and that and this and that and this and
that and this and that and this and that and this and that and this and
that and this and that and this and that and this and that and this and
that and this and that and this and that and this and that and this and
that and this and that and this and that and this and that and this and
that and this and that and this and that and this and that and this and
that and this and that and this and that and this and that and this and
that and this and that and this and that and this and that and this and
that and this and that and this and that and this and that and this and
that and this and that and this and that and this and that and this and
that and this and that and this and that and this and that and this and
that and this and that and this and that and this and that and this and
that and this and that and this and that and this and that and this and
that and this and that and this and that and this and that and this and
that and this and that and this and that and this and that and this and
that and this and that and this and that and this and that and this and
that and this and that and this and that and this and that and this and
that and this and that and this and that and this and that and this and
that and this and that and this and that and this and that and this and
that and this and that and this and that and this and that and this and
that and this and that and this and that and this and that and this and
that and this and that and this and that and this and that and this and
that and this and that and this and that and this and that and this and
that and this and that and this and that and this and that and this and
that and this and that and this and that and this and that and this and
that and this and that and this and that and this and that and this and
that and this and that and this and that and this and that and this and
that and this and that and this and that and this and that and this and
that and this and that and this and that and this and that and this and
that Sind this and that and this and that and this and that and this and
that and this and that and this and that and this and that and this and
that and this and that and this and that and this and that and this and
that and this and that and this and that and this and that and this and
that and this and that and this and that and this and that and this and
that and this and that and this and that and this and that and this and
that and this and that and this and that and this and that and this and

We'll stop the heart
for one minute and electrocute it.
Hopefully it beats
at regular intervals.

///

You can't just eat sugars all day.
"If I die, I die."
If you die, I die.
I break the heart before
it begins to work backwards.

///

"I think I'm going to start meditating
but I don't want to be the one who meditates
I'm already the one who writes poetry."

She began to reverse in time, seeing all of her loved ones spring back
to life. It was hard to dig up their graves, but when she found their
bodies, they recomposed. Flesh flew back to bones. She cried again
and again until the world blurred.

\\\

I was insane and I imagined everything, right up to your existence. It
was all just a delusion. Your life. Your death.

///

We raced down the hill on
my bike, the purple
banana seat holding the two
of us, trusted in gravity
and rode until knees
were bloody with hope.

///

Lyrically speaking, i just can't stop talking about myself.

///

"11. Talk to yourself." –
DZ: How is persistence?
DZ: I am marked by the inexistent.
DZ: When we talk about life, do you feel the question on your
shoulder?
DZ: Ambiguous statements are a defence mechanism.
DZ: Why?
DZ: Well, oh you know, there is this and that.

///

"As your teen's understanding about death evolves, questions may
naturally come up about mortality and vulnerability."

///

"13. Keep a journal of what makes you anxious."
The border between civility and anarchy, the lines between your skin,
fitting this body into the earth, fitting, fit, finishing, the fear of forever,
infinity, how we become the body or the body becomes us, I can't stop
drinking smoothies, protein me, you have your eyes on someone else
and there is a point where I become invisible, goodbye, or goodbyes,
or every time you step into a car there is the possibility that you
will need to be cut out of it, the first, the second, being the last, the
meaning of love or the word, the cyclical nature of existence, how we
end, how we end, how we end, how we end.

\\\

You were calling us to tell us you were OK. I asked my sisters and
they told me that you called. I was failing art class and social studies.
I couldn't get out of bed. Someone reminded me that you were dead,
but I remembered the calls. And then I didn't remember the calls. I
had made it up; you never called. Nadia came over and insisted you
had written a letter for us and had it mailed to our table one dinner.
We opened the letter; it was the size of a fridge. It wasn't your writing.
I had fictionalized your life after death, the way I always do.

///

There is so much of the body we do not dissect
start and end with the eyes.

///

But the words come back each morning as if said in the present. And
the pain came back, the very next day.

\\\

I was holding you, and you couldn't walk. You threw up from the pain.
The elevator went up and up and up and we never got off, there was no
floor for you. The hospital was empty. I told you that I knew you were
dead and I'd wake up soon. You apologized.

///

"Label your fears from 0 to 10."

///

I thought I saw you, walking down the street. You were laughing at your own joke, as you always did. I thought I saw you, but that was just me watching the past go by.

///

> When you were gone
> I had to run across
> the dark spans before
> the night would stop
> hailing cherry blossoms
> and pulling me down.

When you were gone
I had to run across
the dark spans before
the night would stop
but the cherry blossoms
they bury me.

///

They tell me that this world is the same, it's the one you used to be in, but I can tell something is different. Something is wrong, and I'll wake up.

I'M TAKING A SOCIAL MEDIA BREAK!!!

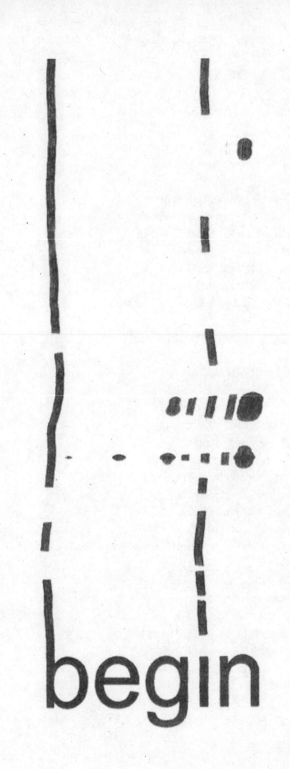

begin

LOL JK I'M DEAD

I am here today to let you know that
lol, I am dead.
jk, I was never dead, lol. What I mean to say
is lol, jk or more specifically jk lol.
I'm not dead
Christopher Meloni is dead, jk lol
I once had a sex dream with Christopher Meloni
and he held me on the shore of a lake
as the moon lay low to the earth
and lit up the sky, and he said
that this meant the world to him
but could never happen again
then I died lol
I'm taking a social media break!!!
Delete that.
I took the Tide Pod challenge and I
literally died.
jk. I lol'd once and then I died. jk
I'm dying I screamed although I
wasn't really dying or screaming.
If you put every embarrassing
moment you had in childhood
end to end, you could stretch
the length of your pants being
pulled down on a football field.
jk, lol-ify your life! Text "I don't feel good lol" or "I can't
leave my bed lol."
Delete that. H&M is really really sorry
I know because they promoted
their tweet to apologize, and I
a true consumer of apologies, accepted.
lol. I am dead. jk! Today I all-capsed
at everyone on the internet, please
please @ me.

When this all ends, I just want
you to put me deep within the earth
below a gravestone that reads
lol, jk, I am dead.
In that
exact
order.

I LOVE YOU A.C. SLATER

1.
A.C. Slater glides into the room
he smiles, dimples
break you in two
you are in love, he shoots
a finger gun at you.

2.
Shawn runs his hands
through his hair, split
perfectly into two parts.
There are these two parts
to his hair, it parts
you in two.

3.
Uncle Jesse cries
in the storage room
of The Smash Club
you are sitting across from him.
He tells you it's too much
to leave her, but he will.

4.
The Red Ranger
holds out his arms
yells "T. Rex"
and becomes
you.

5.
A.C. Slater
in his wrestling
unitard.

6.
If you split me down the middle.

7.
Prayer isn't as effective
as you think. He
cannot split into two.

8.
Before I would go to bed
I used to whisper every word
I could think of, wondering
if each word was the word
to Mighty Morph. That each person
can unlock their powers with
the right word. I still believe this
to be true.

9.
Harvey doesn't know
about your secret life
the secret attic door
that goes into a world
he can't accept. Salem
is a cat who talks, but
that's a different secret.

10.
You put all of your thoughts
in A.C. Slater's dimples
the one about him
the one that splits you into two
the word you use
to morph into something else.

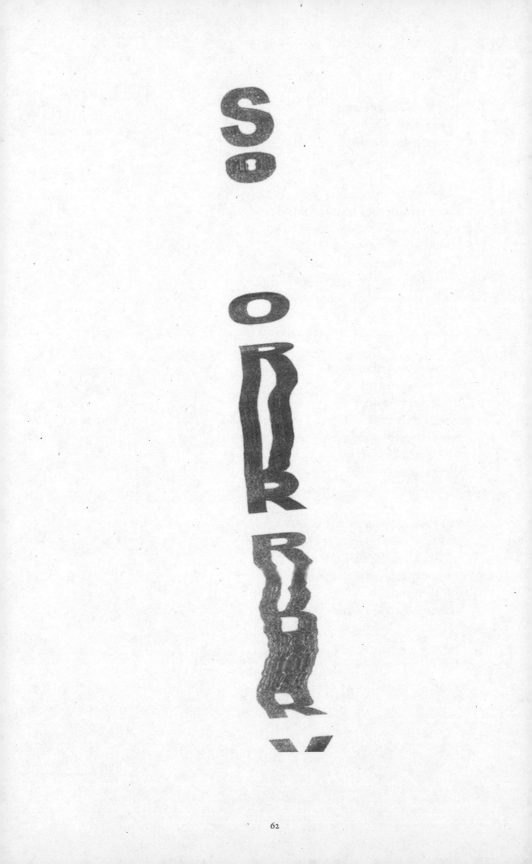

I WENT ONLINE TO GET MY FEELINGS HURT

When I was younger, the family computer
filled up with so many porn viruses
that my mother yelled at me
for ruining the computer
but when bouncy breasts filled
the screen in each new
pop-up
I pretended it was me.

Now I go online to
make friends with the people
who hate me most!

"Bert and Ernie aren't for you
you disgusting faggot."
He tweets.

Did you ever upload floppy dicks
on to floppy disks? No? Take the *Friends* quiz
who would be your potential partner?

Sometimes being anonymous
online feels like I can be as large as
the world, or as small as an atom
I prefer to be an atom.

When I was younger I HTML'd on *Matrix*
message boards and thought I was
building friendships but they suspended
my accounts when they found out I
had several I would use
to talk to myself.

I do think Bert and Ernie
are for me.

When I was thirteen I
had a GeoCities site

called Daniel's House Party
that was just MIDI files of
Jamiroquai songs and GIFs of disco balls.
I wanted to know what it was like
to have friends to dance with
to disappear in a crowd.
I would turn the lights off and stare
into the screen, bopping my head
wiggling my legs, on here I am
a dance party, I am Morpheus
I am dating Ross, and I am
waiting for the computer
to swallow me up.

follow me

follow me

follow me

follow me

follow me

SELFIE

When you were alive, I hid behind
you in a photo, to protect myself.

Someone told me that a photo
takes something away from you

and I believed them, so there is
this photo of you, with my tiny

legs poking behind. I still
hate having my photo taken.

THE SIMS 2: EXPANSION PACK

Build a home. Start small, something
just for your simple necessities.

You never really needed much
anyway, just a bed, a kitchen

a small TV for when you're
tired of reading books. Then

you meet someone, a neighbour
you're not really sure about.

He has slicked-back-90s-dad hair
and his square walk reminds you

of the way you walk. Rigid, with
quick turns of corner. He starts

coming over more than you expected
so you start buying more things

for your house. You upgrade your
stereo and your TV, and

maybe a palm tree outside, because
you're a fun guy with whimsy.

He comes over one day, and you
have a heart-shaped hot tub

waiting in your bedroom.
He comes in, a little hesitantly.

This is when you right-click your
move, and go in for the kiss.

Hands wave "No, no, no!" in the air.
You try again, and this time he

lets hearts burst from his head.
Your bodies turn to blurry pixels

and in moments it's all over.
He puts his clothes on.

You can see him from your window now
roaming his kitchen, forgetting.

DON'T WORRY IT'S NOT LOADED

i'd kill myself but Obama took all our guns and turned them into gay bars.
—Anonymous Commenter

I went to the firing range and it turned out to be a gay bar, and every
single gun was not a gun but a gay bar. I immigrated to America
before a civil war broke out and before anyone could bear arms
they were baring ass in a gay bar and they pointed their gay bars at
each other. My neighbour asked us if we were going to get a gay bar,
because there were like fifty thousand gay bars sold in California
during a pandemic and I thought, I just don't want to own a gay bar.
Well, just not in my home. Imagine if that gay bar went off by accident,
or if someone broke in and used the gay bar against us. I heard gay
bars were not being sold at Walmart anymore. In Canada there are
more rules around gay bars but people definitely still own gay bars.
        What if you bought a gun and it turned into a gay bar? You
    pulled on the trigger and it just made you wait in line. What if you
        bought a gun and it turned into a gay bar and a drag queen made
    you take a shot and shook your head between her breasts? What if
    you bought a gun and it turned into a gay bar and it exploded with
confetti? What if you bought a gun and it turned into a gay bar and we
                    got totally loaded and danced until last call?

FRANKENSTEIN'S MONSTER VS. DRACULA[1] VS. ME

Cold blue water was between me.
"Do you think I wanted to be evil?" the monster asked.
A terrible desire came upon me.
I was afraid that the monster would leave. "Stay," I said.

The monster looked at me in surprise.
The waves rose in growing fury, each over-topping its fellow
till in a very few minutes the lately glassy sea was roaring and devouring.
He seems alive only when he talks of his hunt.

The monster stared at me.
So I asked him point-blank, "Why may I not go tonight?"
I could hear a lot of words often repeated, queer words.
I remember hearing the sudden barking of the dogs like praying on a
very tumultuous scale.

When the monster finished his story, I didn't know what to say.
A terrible desire.
It seems like a profanation of the word
to write it in connection with such a monster.

When I saw him at his own place he looked queer.
I did not sleep well, though my bed was comfortable enough.
The decanter of sherry was on the table half-full.
"Let me go, you monster!" he cried.

I had created the monster
and this was very much on my mind.
He would see me only as an ugly monster.
"I know why you think that," the monster said.

---

1   Text pulled from *Frankenstein; or, The Modern Prometheus* by Mary Shelley and
     Dracula by Bram Stoker

Commented [DZ1]: Why do you always find yourself in an ocean, metaphorically speaking?

Commented [DZ2]: The original scraps of this poem sit on your desk back home. You meant to paste them to paper, manufacture meaning.

Commented [DZ3]: You use experimental works to remove the feeling, to produce like a robot; did it work?

Commented [DZ4]: The scraps sit on your desk at home, you jumped in a car and drove through the night because she was in the hospital again.

Commented [DZ5]: You don't pray anymore.

Commented [DZ6]: You both watch whatever is on TV, flip through, start a season, one more episode, one more episode, one more.

Commented [DZ7]: You don't actually believe in monsters, not anymore. No one person filled with evil, just circumstances that make monsters of us all.

Commented [DZ8]: You googled how long Ativan lasts in case you needed to drive to the hospital.

Commented [DZ9]: The real monster is at a cellular level, taking over a body, one by one.

Commented [DZ10]: You updated her calendar to the present date when you made it to the apartment so it didn't feel like ten days in hospital.

I had learned from the monster.
Because the monster lives alone, I must also live alone.
Then, in a second, he was gone
Is he not a monster for doing that?

I found one last note from the monster.
The monster saw what I did.
I knew now well enough
I cannot love again.

I must destroy the monster.

Commented [DZ11]: You write this as she rests on the couch, she doesn't quite understand the experimental part of the poem, you're bad at explaining that.

Commented [DZ12]: You light the Christmas tree once more before you take it down. Light candles. Start another show.

Commented [DZ13]: You write this as she rests on the couch, deep in the desert, far far away from the ocean.

Commented [DZ14]: The scraps sit on your desk at home, you change the calendar date by a day, one more, one more, one more, one more …

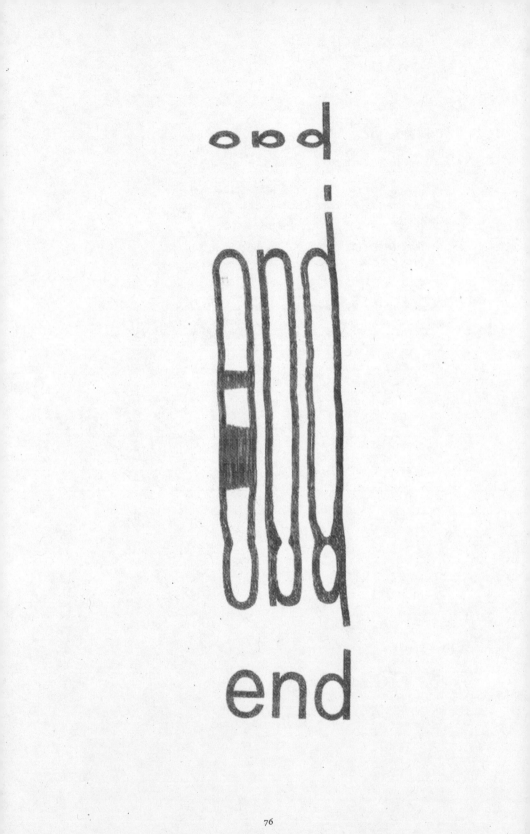

end

"WHAT'S YOUR FAVOURITE SCARY MOVIE?"

JUMP SCARE

A quiet suburb bubbles
in the background when

a kid gets choked
from behind and

we pull back to reveal
a hole in the ground

it opens until the world
falls into it, then you appear.

You move into a new home
where the furnace wheezes

in the basement. A wind whispers
in the attic, it knows your name

the only one that talks to you
in an empty home.

Voices call out goodnight
as the day slips away.

You talk back to them
everyone says you talk in your sleep.

A mirror can only do so much
to take you down

show a body that fits
poorly into the shape you imagined

one day my sisters showed me that
if you say Bloody Mary's name three times

in a mirror in the dark with
only candlelight she will come

take you, slice your body in
two and return to her other world in the mirror.

When my sisters were away
I tried alone

eyes turned red I
flicked the lights on to banish her

each night
I would hold onto wake

staring at the mirror
in the bedroom

until too late
worried in the night

I would say the words
times three and

she would come
to take another sister away.

If you fail an introduction class
for swimming three times, it should be
illegal to let a kid swim
or let a drunk teen near a body of water.

In class, they ask you to lie
flat
            and float.
Water filled
my eye sockets and my body
dropped to the ground. My tiny
garbage lungs only willing to fill up
with enough air to slowly drown.

Take the darkest path to
the body of water, the white spokes
of trees lining the path
to teens drunk in the night.

A body of water is supposed to let a body
of mostly water and Baja Rosa
float.

Baja Rosa, a strawberry tequila liquor
can be slammed in about three minutes
at a bonfire if the cops are coming.

Down here, we all float.

When the boys splashed
puddles at my face I laughed
they flicked mud water
with hockey sticks like
prayer like blessing like
baptism until I dropped.

Did they hope the never-ending
mud water would clean me
or erase desire? Or maybe they
knew I couldn't float and wanted
me to sink.

I always think of drowning
sinking, of the stones in my body
dropping me to the bottom of the lake.
I think of feet that wash ashore, how
a body of water can take us apart
like a puzzle.

Pennywise would come too. Take
up the space of our sewers, light
them up, and pull me down.

Give me a red balloon

                    let me float.

Don't run down into the basement
don't be silly, there's no way out, it's just cement

and open walls, exposed wood
2 × 4s lined with nails, it's

all stolen toys from Sears and text
books, cut knees and concussions

hum and roar from the furnace
and kissing boys who will

pretend this never happened and memory
and loss and vomit and if you

ever fucking tell someone and
Bloody Mary, Bloody Mary
Bloody Mary, and eyes
turning red

and bright purple
blisters, turn the lights on!

Dear Michael Myers
I wanted to congratulate you on your forty-year work
anniversary on LinkedIn but we are no longer linked

I wanted to say your commitment is unwavering, to being blown up
to be kicked, beaten but still return to your hometown

Michael, we have a lot in common like
I'm a slow walker with hyperfixations

Michael, I was thinking the other day, have you ever
thought retiring early
could be nice, or maybe a job at a tech start-up
could fulfill your bloody desires
no one will notice you wear the same outfit every day
and everyone is tortured

if we network together would you feel love in some form
at first I didn't think of it when you unblocked me

but I wanted to really nourish the wedge growing between us
turning it into an infected pit in my stomach,
call it Pitty or Cavity, something cute
what if the rage I give in my replies is just as intimate as a like

do you have an online persona
that attacks teens when they least expect it, what's your avi

DEBATE ME

I used to troll people too, very unforgiving work

if you had Grindr would you have a face pic
an endless bio explaining all the things you don't desire

or is a body a body a body

does the sight of endless torsos
 feel like you've brought your work home with you
do you read Reddit before bed, do you think you're the victim here

Dear Michael, if you take off your mask
I'll take off mine

Did you lock the doors
did you check three times

when you awake
does the nightmare still

cover the body
slick with salted memory

did you peel back
memory

like tendon from the bone
is someone in the house

is he invited
did you let him in

did he charm the door
open as monsters do

A demon has tagged you in a post
"The faggots are out" he types

and guess what? He's right! We rise
I started reading the bible and
got bored, you said you would
make me and all of my friends
pay for our sins and I just thought
it was really nice of you to
think that I had friends or honestly
think of me at all.

Tag me again, and again
add another threat, a thread
needle through, pop out of
my phone and surprise me!

I think so much about the thread
how it connects us, when one of
us pulls away, a tear. Holes in
every inch of our skin, making
Pinhead jealous.

After your account
was deleted, I waited
you spawned again.
Tag me, start a new thread
everyone loves a
sequel.

Long-nail fingers slide the door open
scratching the walls.
Freddy lies back and looks in the mirror.

He looks awkward, shifts over, slices
his sweater to show a little chest. Arches
his back. Flicks his needle-point fingers in the air
whispers, "ugly."

He flips around onto his belly, kicks his legs up
puts his finger to his lip, cuts it a little.

A glowing light beams through the heating vent
the light grows, turns from a small spider
to a large buck-toothed clown.

Freddy slices pompoms
off Pennywise's shirt, cuts his pants
from the waist, screams at his crotch
"Beep Beep Richie!"

Pennywise lifts Freddy up by his chin
whispers "What do you want to see?"
Freddy nods in a way that lets Penny know
it's what he always wants to see.

It opens his chest until it becomes
a cave that becomes a small town
where the children lie awake
every night, where it never turns dark
where he no longer exists.

This is where they say we should
split up, even though you beg them

to stick around. But there is only
so long they can stay, better

split up, see where this goes
let your best friend, your boyfriend

your sisters, your father, your mother
go on without you.

We start with everyone, every single
person and we split up, cut in half

split down the earth, split
divide like atoms, until

it's just one of us in every room
in this haunted house.

Jigsaw shows up, again and again
and we are all connected
the entire earth's population
by a fine cord and any sudden move
will take us all out
during a gender reveal party.

Queers go missing under
the city, through a water duct
by way of Pennywise

cities wash them down
with rainwater, and no one
asks where they went

queers go missing, and
the news passes by
like a stream.

Pennywise came to you
as a red balloon offering a
a place of comfort

you went missing
and I looked everywhere
for you the cops didn't

queers get swallowed
up in a city that thinks all
lost souls end up in

a place we built
a place where evil
is just your imagination.

I didn't follow you back on Instagram
because you burned the whole school down
and I felt it was problematic.

It's the memories that keep you
up at night, not the nightmares

the jump scare is the men
who followed you out the club

or the jump scare is the car
you drove into the night

or the jump scare is the memory
that relocates itself in the bones

or we watch
as a

clown jumps from a projector
she drops from your ceiling

he appears on the third try
a hand punches out of a grave

knife plunges through a curtain
an alien bursts through body

Jason leaps from the water
you crawl from the TV screen

thrash at the closet
come through the mirror

your head rips
through my stomach

intestines dangling from
your face.

Dear Freddy,

If you're here please let me know
it feels as if I'm trying to conjure you.

Nightmare me
watch as my family surrounds me
my last breaths time like a clock
mouth ajar. I look over my casket
smaller than me, with only a few flowers.
You laugh and ask if I am scared yet.
Freddy, I asked you to keep the funeral small
not the casket.
Little monsters burble up
from the fireplace, Christmas tree
burned to crisp, I can't breathe. You ask if I'm scared yet.
Trapped in the underworld, unspool
ribbon from my throat
bury me alive. Stuck in an asylum
I can't find the exit. I put on
a wet sweater and it traps
around my face. Rip my chest open
and climb inside!
This plane is crashing
dinner party is unplanned, the
world collapses in on itself, bombs
go off and border walls go up
guns pop, daily mass shootings, Freddy
is this what you dream of?

Awake, I will ask if this is real
if the pit in my stomach is you, Freddy, if the gut
feeling of failure, of doom, is just synapses
firing in the night, if the glove on your hand
protects you from the cold
if you sharpen the blades every morning. Dear Freddy
do you miss me
when I can't sleep?

She dangles the keys
there's no escape

it didn't drown, instead
it still follows you

tongue click
pull the ghost face mask off

aren't we all a little mad
sometimes

it was you all along
walking backwards

calling the demons
telling them only seven days

contorting your body
to satiate a monster

are you still
hungry?

who will save you
from yourself?

They all logged out and
it was only you on a screen, you

alone in a house, each left through
the door or a window, you

in a forest with the only whispers
from wind between trees, you

silent under the bed, shh
hold your breath, you

in the cabin in the woods
staring into the corner, you

wondering where they all went
how they figured out an exit.

If this is the end? Then
fuck it, Freddy

meet me at the altar
in the basement

find me in the woods
I'm waiting.

Freddy, when she called you faggot
did you like the taste of those words

in your mouth? The blood glistening
on teeth – just corn syrup.

Can you find me? A nobody
knows how to be invisible.

Freddy, these nightmares you
gifted, honey

Gwyneth Paltrow trying to murder
me in my mother's house again? Really?

Bored now. Bury the monsters
in the backyard again, bury

the curse in a cavity, bludgeon
the fears until forgiveness

burn in a house
of your own making

let the fucking gods
come take this place back.

When I take your glove and plunge
the blades into your gut, does it tickle?

Goodbye, dear Freddy
you will be missed.

double tap because they
always come back.

Blood dries as you stumble
down the empty street

you and the sun rising
are all that is left.

Credits roll
text slips up screen

like water ripples
in the dead of night.

I don't want to write another
poem, just lie

in the basement
float on an ocean

of cold
cement.

When I assume it's all over
a red balloon floats up

and I wait for you and I wait for you
and I wait for you.

OK BYE!!!

I guess the moment that things really changed was when the world turned to globs. We were driving back from a road trip with our dog and it felt as if we hit a big bump in the road and then everything – the cars, the trees, our bodies – all turned to jelly. Just rolling and bouncing around. Things flopped against other things and bits and gloops slapped each other around and mixed – a bit of you squished with me and a bit of me glopped onto them. The speed of our car kept our booger-bodies going, the earth slick, a waterslide with no traction. At some point along the drive, our globs separated but there were still bits of each other there. And more people globbed on. I could tell a bit of the dog was here, too. And I rolled and rolled, growing bigger and sometimes smaller, watching the bubbles of blood and bone and skin pass by. I gathered bits of my old home as I passed it, the floorboards dipping into my liver and my esophagus. This happened for years, just gathering bits and bits until each glob had a bit of every person and thing, until each of us was a milkshake of guts and dirt and junk. Until finally most of me reached the sea and dispersed into the water like oil, floating into the ocean. Then sun roasted us as we crusted over, turning to flakes and clusters of clumped dust. My elbow scattered next to the eyes of the dog, my head cemented into part of a steering wheel. My butt spread across the beach like icing. My heart clumped with yours. Our little world, a perfect pavlova.

ABOUT THE POEMS

"Nobody!" was published in *a fine. collection, vol. I.*

"how to get washboard abs – fast" is an ongoing poem that has been published in various forms and excerpts in *Why Poetry Sucks: An Anthology of Humorous Experimental Canadian Poetry, Flicker and Spark: A Contemporary Queer Anthology of Spoken Word and Poetry, Plentitude,* and on my Tumblr account. It is incomplete and rewritten every year or so. It will be rewritten again.

"I Literally Feel Bad All of the Time LOL" is a compilation of several poems written over the last fifteen years, excerpts of which have been published in *Witches Magazine* and on Craigslist Missed Connections and Tumblr. It covers the process I went through from trying to understand my anxiety disorder diagnosis to the present day with my autism diagnosis. Some text was scrambled from online autism tests along with other material, but the main test is sourced from this site: www.additudemag.com/reviews/post/screener-autism-spectrum-disorder-symptoms-test-adults/.

"He Drags Her Body, or Working Backwards," for my mother and sister, is also a never-ending poem; as with grief, I will revisit it, add to it, edit it as time goes on. Some of the text comes from these articles on grief and anxiety and panic attacks along with text that no longer exists on the internet: sg.theasianparent.com/how-to-talk-to-your-child-about-death, www.thehealthy.com/mental-health/anxiety/deal-with-anxiety-and-get-your-life-back/, www.ipc-mn.com/10-golden-rules-for-coping-with-panic-attacks/.

"I Love You A.C. Slater" was published in *Contemporary Verse 2* magazine.

"Selfie" was published in *Here & Now: An Anthology of Queer Italian-Canadian Writing.*

In the poem "Don't Worry It's Not Loaded," the anonymous comment, "i'd kill myself but Obama took all our guns and turned them into gay bars" was sourced from a queer article that has since been deleted.

"Frankenstein's Monster vs. Dracula vs. Me" was published on *Undecimals*.

Excerpts of "Jump Scare" were published in *Prism* magazine. The recommended viewing for this long poem is: the *A Nightmare on Elm Street* franchise, *Freddy vs. Jason*, *It* (both versions), *It Follows*, *Get Out*, *Hereditary*, *Midsommar*, *The Ring*, the *Halloween* franchise, *The Cabin in the Woods*, *Carrie* (original), *Alien*, *Saw* (honestly the first one is enough), *The Strangers*, the *Scream* franchise, *Unfriended*, *Host*, the *Friday the 13th* franchise, *Candyman*, *Hellraiser*, *The Babadook*, *Happy Birthday to Me*, and *Prom Night*.

ACKNOWLEDGMENTS

Thank you to my first readers Dina Del Bucchia and Gabe Liedman. Dina, who always puts in so much time and effort with my writing and is always up for happy hour. And Gabe, who always has something kind to say about my words and keeps me from losing my shit, A+ husband. Thank you to David Ly and Brad Aaron Modlin for editorial notes and for being delightful writers.

Thank you to Talonbooks for taking this book on: Catriona Strang for her thoughtful and attentive notes, and Kevin Williams, Vicki Williams, Spencer Williams, Charles Simard, Erin Kirsh, Leslie Smith, Darren Atwater, Sophie Collis, and Rya the dog, who continue to make Talonbooks a wonderful space for poets.

Thank you to my family, Diana, Julia, Kevin, Frank, Nicholas, Alyssa, Lucca, Eva, and to my extended family, Julie, Amy, Eli, Meera, Grey, and Lilia. And thank you to the rest of my family, which would take me too many pages to list. Thank you to our dog Lidia for bringing absolute havoc in our lives and for napping alongside me as I write. Thank you to my mother Simira, Tina, Nonna, and Nella; while you're not physically here on this earth anymore, you still are there for me when I need you.

This book was written over many, many years and these poems would not exist without every single person who has come in and out of my life, even for a brief moment. To name them would be way too much work and I'm too afraid I would miss someone if I did.

And, as always, thank you, for reading this book.

DANIEL ZOMPARELLI is the founder of *Poetry Is Dead* magazine. He founded the magazine while working at *Adbusters* in 2009. He is a former co-podcaster at *Can't Lit* along with Dina Del Bucchia. His first book of poems, *Davie Street Translations*, was published by Talonbooks in 2012. His poems and writing have been anthologized and published around the world. His collaborative book with Dina Del Bucchia, *Rom Com*, was published by Talonbooks in 2015. His collection of short stories, *Everything Is Awful and You're a Terrible Person*, was nominated for the Ethel Wilson Fiction Prize and won the ReLit Short Fiction Award. It has been translated into German, French, and Spanish. His podcast *I'm Afraid That* was listed as one of the best podcasts of 2018 by *Esquire* and featured as a podcast to listen to on A/V Club and BBC America. He recently edited *Queer Little Nightmares*, published by Arsenal Pulp Press, with David Ly. He currently lives in Los Angeles.

PHOTO: Victoria Black